Now you... tenor saxoph... specially rec... ...ngements

TAKE THE LEAD

tenor saxophone

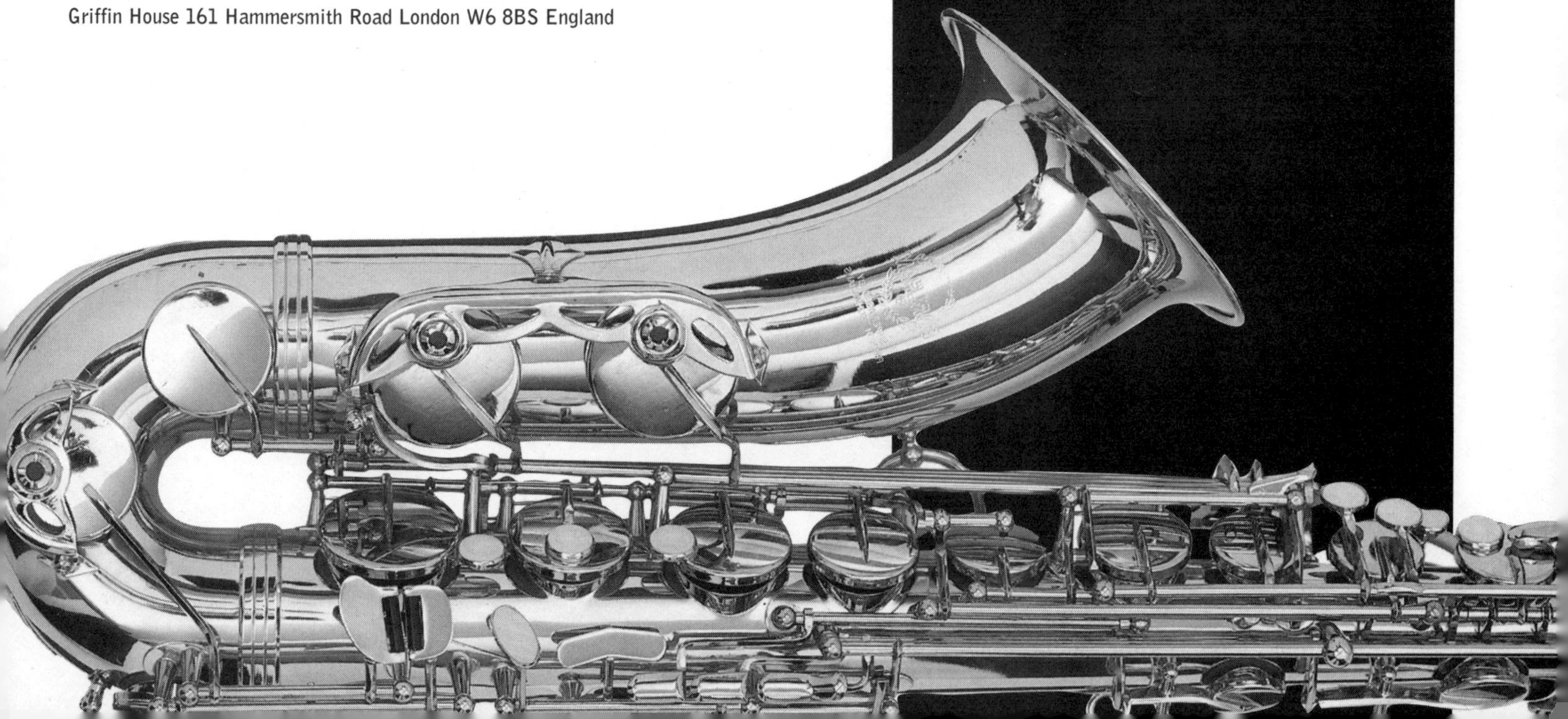

IMP
International MUSIC Publications

International Music Publications Limited
Griffin House 161 Hammersmith Road London W6 8BS England

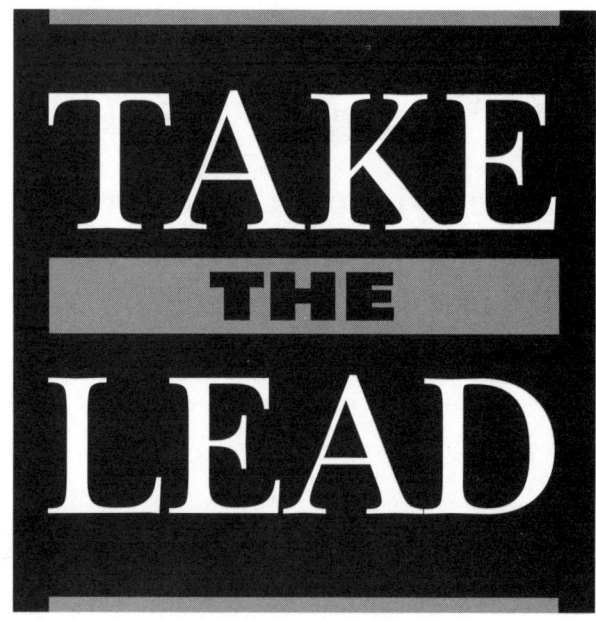

DON'T BE A MUSIC COPYCAT!

The copying of © copyright material is a criminal offence and may lead to prosecution.

Series Editors: Sadie Cook and Miranda Steel

Editorial, production and recording: Artemis Music Limited
Design and production: Space DPS Limited

Published 2000

International MUSIC Publications

© International Music Publications Limited
Griffin House 161 Hammersmith Road London W6 8BS England

Reproducing this music in any form is illegal and forbidden by the Copyright, Designs and Patents Act 1988

International Music Publications Limited

England: Griffin House
161 Hammersmith Road
London W6 8BS

Germany: Marstallstr. 8
D-80539 München

Denmark: Danmusik
Vognmagergade 7
DK1120 Copenhagen K

Carisch

Italy: Via Campania 12
20098 San Giuliano Milanese
Milano

Spain: Magallanes 25
28015 Madrid

France: 20 Rue de la Ville-l'Eveque
75008 Paris

tenor saxophone

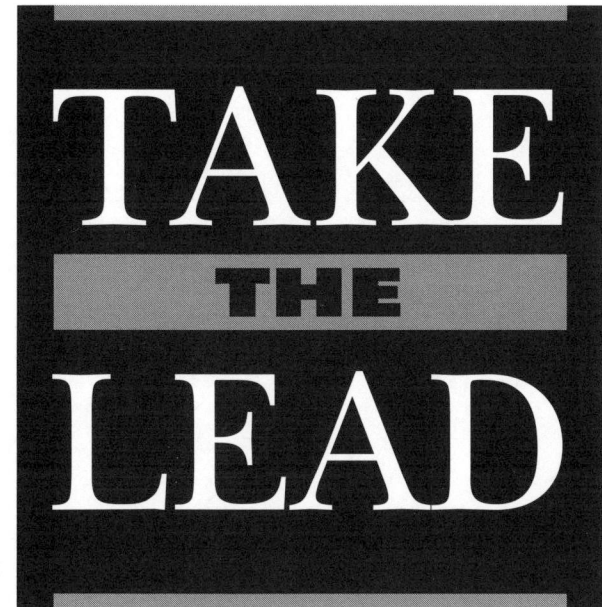

TAKE THE LEAD

In the Book...

Chattanooga Choo Choo 6

Choo Choo Ch'Boogie 18

I've Got A Gal In Kalamazoo 8

In The Mood 10

**It Don't Mean A Thing
(If It Ain't Got That Swing)** 14

Jersey Bounce 21

Pennsylvania 6-5000 24

A String Of Pearls 26

On the CD...

Track **1**   Tuning Tones (A Concert)

Chattanooga Choo Choo
Track **2**   Full version

Track **3**   Backing track

I've Got A Gal In Kalamazoo
Track **4**   Full version

Track **5**   Backing track

In The Mood
Track **6**   Full version

Track **7**   Backing track

It Don't Mean A Thing (If It Ain't Got That Swing)
Track **8**   Full version

Track **9**   Backing track

Choo Choo Ch'Boogie
Track **10**   Full version

Track **11**   Backing track

Jersey Bounce
Track **12**   Full version

Track **13**   Backing track

Pennsylvania 6-5000
Track **14**   Full version

Track **15**   Backing track

A String Of Pearls
Track **16**   Full version

Track **17**   Backing track

Demonstration

Backing

Chattanooga Choo Choo

Music by Harry Warren

© 1941 & 2000 EMI Catalogue Partnership and EMI Feist Catalog Inc, USA
Worldwide print rights controlled by Warner Bros Publications Inc/IMP Ltd

     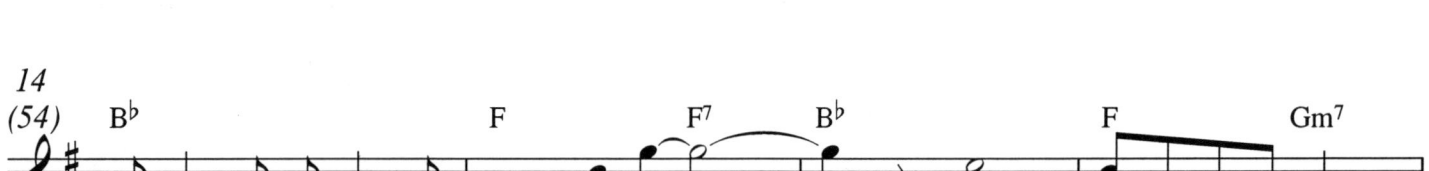 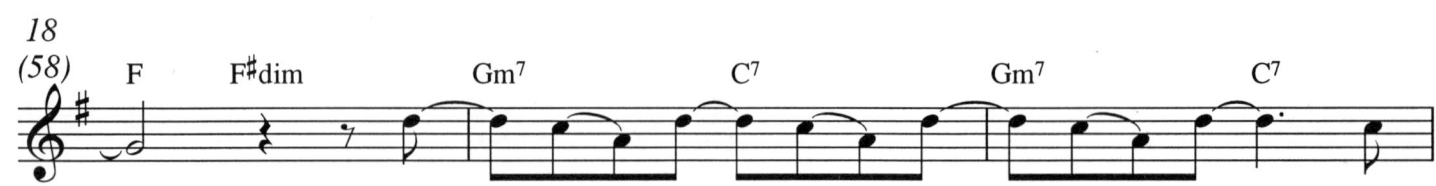 

© 1942 & 2000 Twentieth Century Music Corp and Bregman Vocco & Conn Inc, USA
Warner/Chappell Music Ltd, London W6 8BS

Demonstration Backing

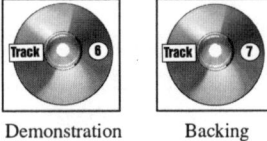

In The Mood

Music by Joe Garland

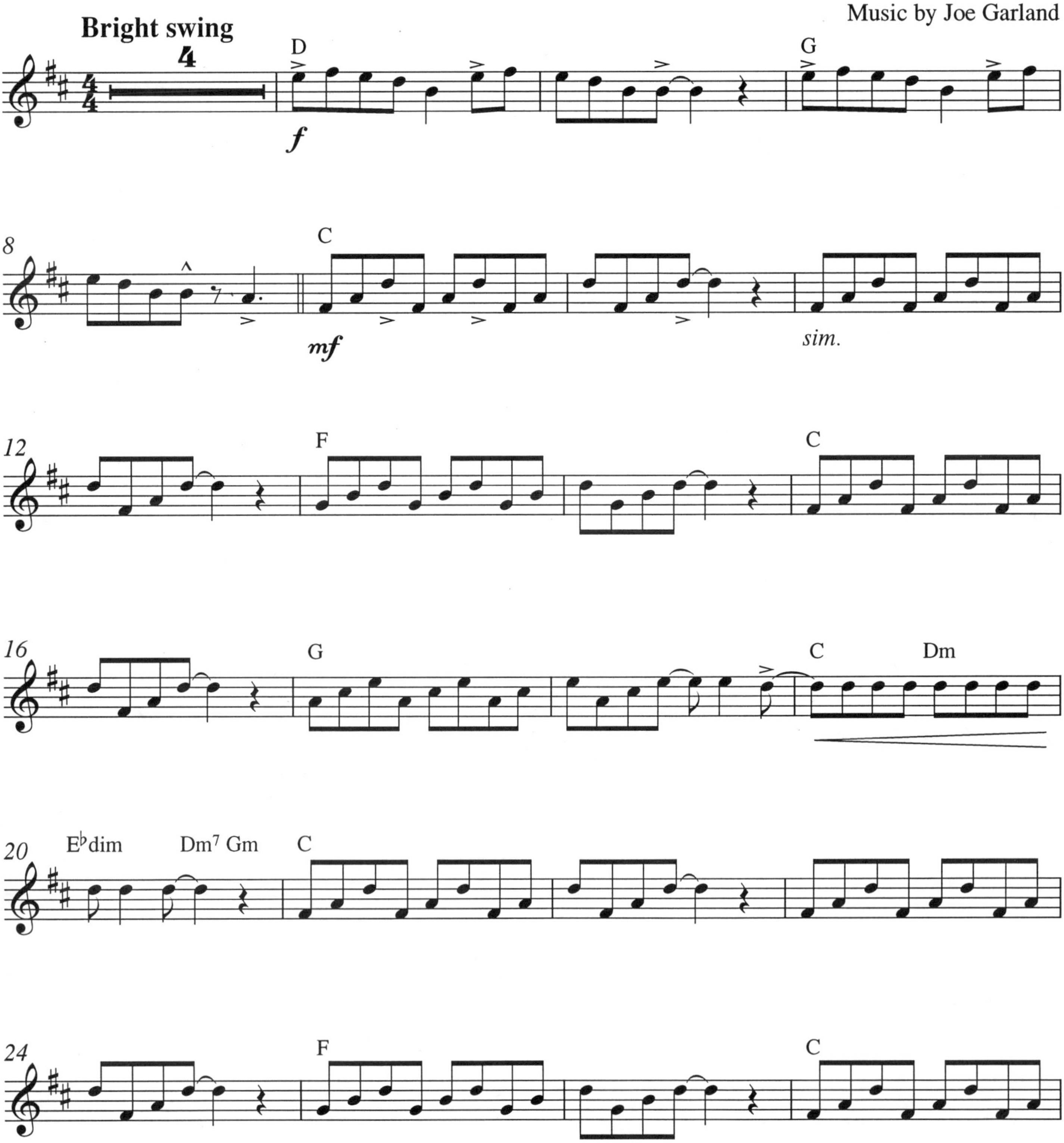

Demonstration

Backing

It Don't Mean A Thing
(If It Ain't Got That Swing)

Music by Duke Ellington

© 1932 & 2000 EMI Mills Music Inc, USA
Worldwide print rights controlled by Warner Bros Publications Inc/IMP Ltd

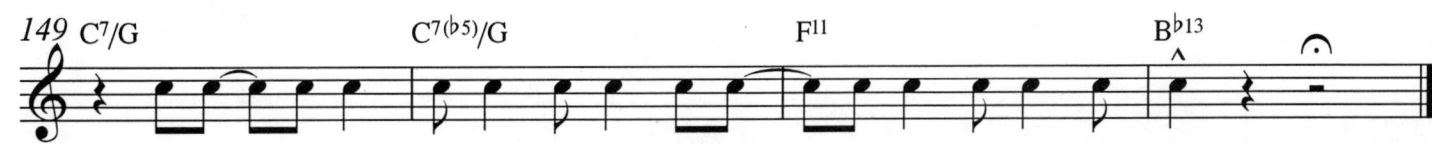

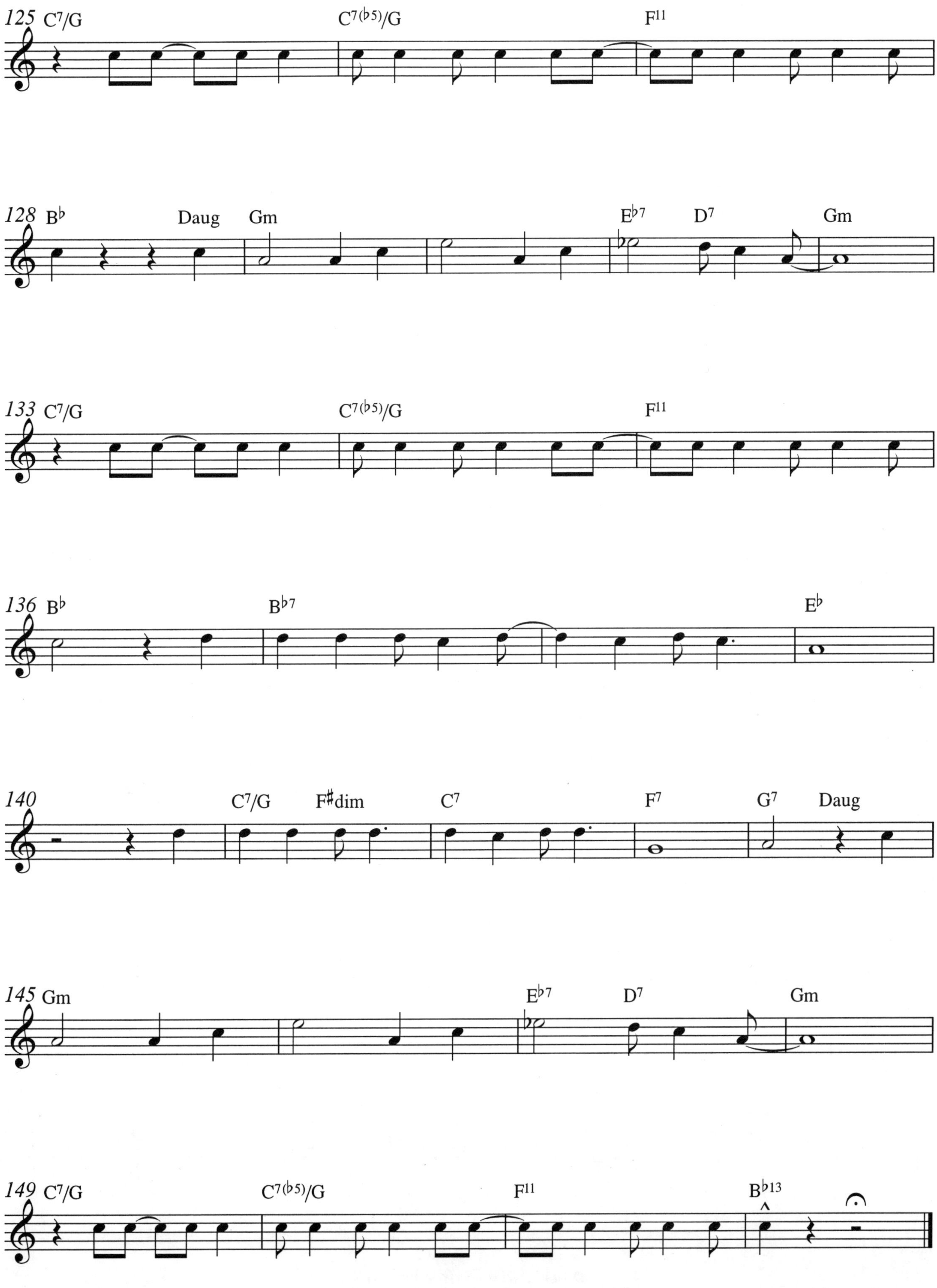
125 C7/G
C7(♭5)/G
F11
128 B♭
Daug
Gm
E♭7
D7
Gm
133 C7/G
C7(♭5)/G
F11
136 B♭
B♭7
E♭
140
C7/G
F♯dim
C7
F7
G7
Daug
145 Gm
E♭7
D7
Gm
149 C7/G
C7(♭5)/G
F11
B♭13

Demonstration

Backing

Choo Choo Ch'Boogie

Words and Music by Denver Darling,
Milton Gabler and Vaughn Horton

Moderate boogie woogie tempo

© 1946 & 2000 Rytvoc Inc, USA
Warner/Chappell Music Ltd, London W6 8BS

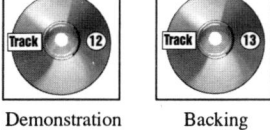

Jersey Bounce

Music by Tiny Bradshaw
and Bobby Plater

Easy swing

© 1941 (renewed) & 2000 Lewis Music Pub Co Inc and Unichappell Music Inc, USA
Warner/Chappell Music Ltd, London W6 8BS

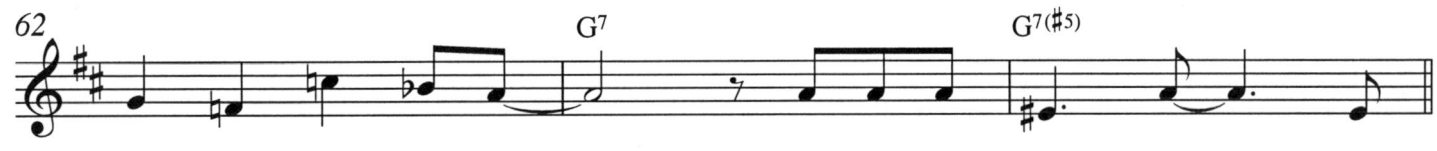

Pennsylvania 6-5000

Music by Jerry Gray

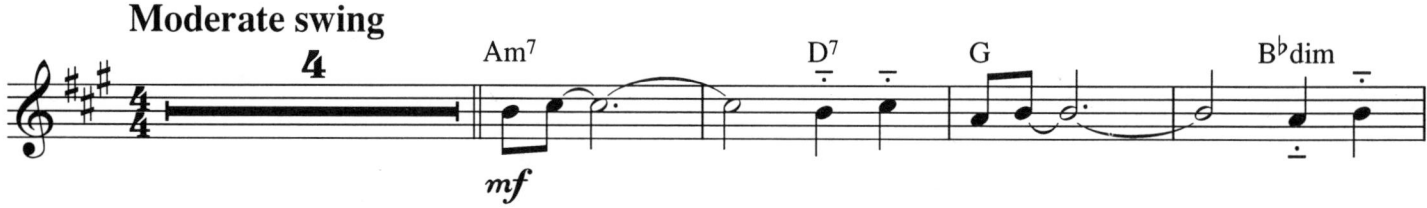

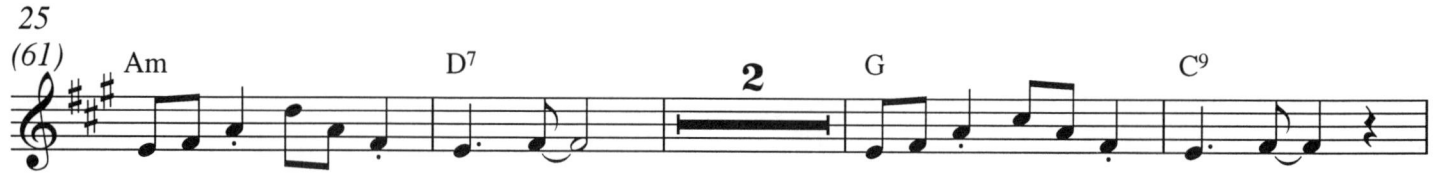

© 1940 & 2000 EMI Catalogue Partnership and EMI Robbins Catalog Inc, USA
Worldwide print rights controlled by Warner Bros Publications Inc/IMP Ltd

Demonstration

Backing

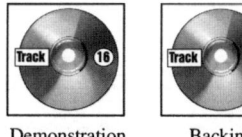

A String Of Pearls

Moderate swing

Music by Jerry Gray

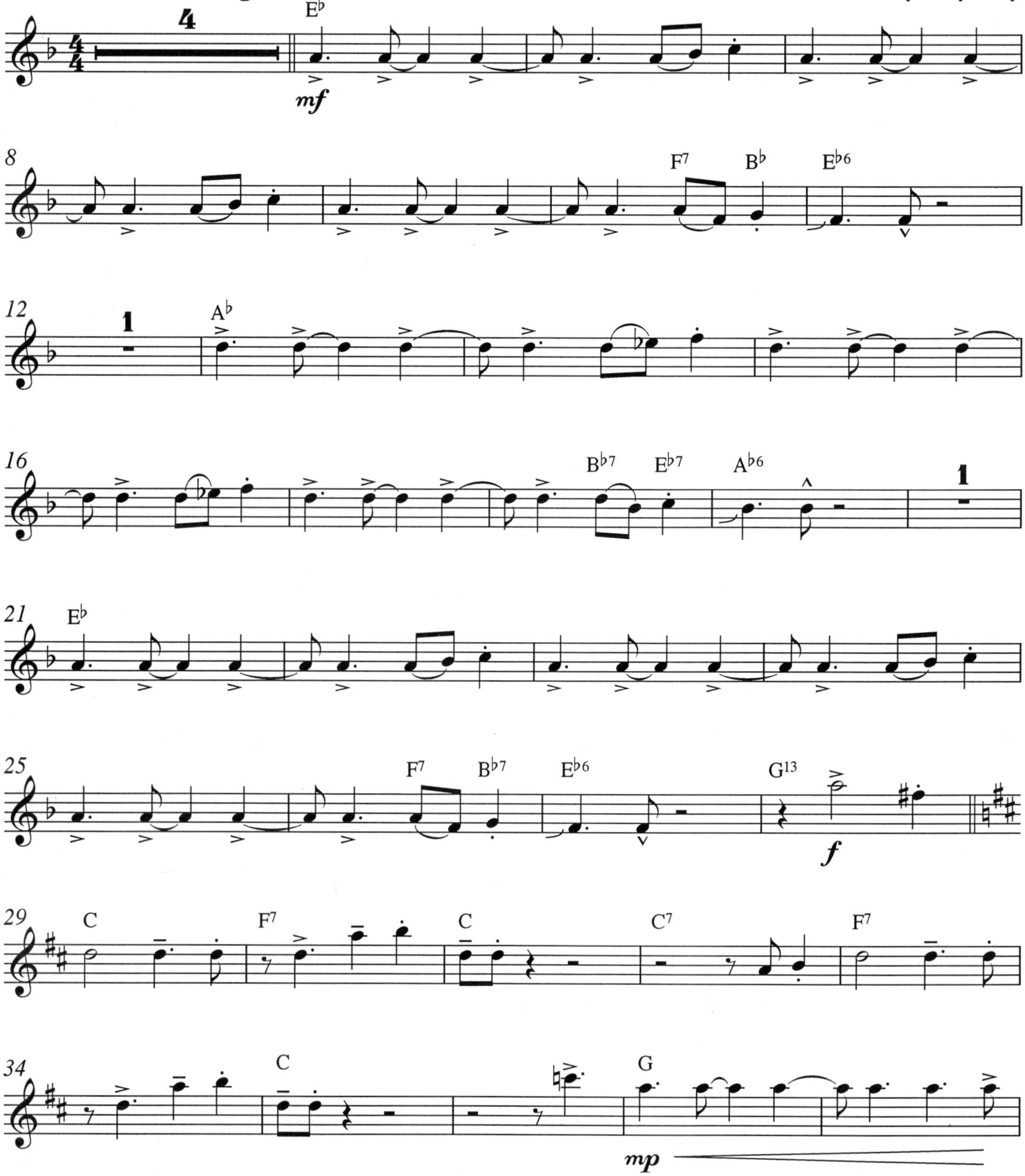